Harriet Tubman

by Dana Meachen Rau

Compass Point Early Biographies

Content Adviser: Professor Sherry L. Field,
Department of Social Science Education, College of Education,
The University of Georgia

Reading Adviser: Dr. Linda D. Labbo,
Department of Reading Education, College of Education,
The University of Georgia

COMPASS POINT BOOKS

Minneapolis, Minnesota

Compass Point Books
3722 West 50th Street, #115
Minneapolis, MN 55410

Visit Compass Point Books on the Internet at *www.compasspointbooks.com* or e-mail your
request to *custserv@compasspointbooks.com*

Photographs ©:

North Wind Picture Archives, cover; Photri-Microstock, 4; Archive Photos, 5; North Wind Picture Archives, 6; Archive Photos,
7, 8, 10, 11; North Wind Picture Archives, 12; Photri-Microstock, 13, 14; Unicorn Stock Photos/Aneal E. Vohra, 15; North Wind
Picture Archives, 16; Archive Photos, 18; Visuals Unlimited/Charles Sykes, 20; Photri-Microstock, 22; Archive Photos, 23;
Schomburg Center/New York Public Library/Astor, Lenox and Tilden Foundations, 24; Archive Photos, 25; Unicorn Stock
Photos/ChromoSohm/Sohm, 26.

Editors: E. Russell Primm and Emily J. Dolbear
Photo Researcher: Svetlana Zhurkina
Photo Selector: Dawn Friedman
Design: Bradfordesign, Inc.

Library of Congress Cataloging-in-Publication Data

Rau, Dana Meachen, 1971–
    Harriet Tubman / by Dana Meachen Rau.
        p. cm. — (Compass Point early biographies)
    Includes bibliographical references and index.
    Summary: An introduction to the life of Harriet Tubman, who helped hundreds of slaves escape to
freedom via the Underground Railroad.
    ISBN 0-7565-0015-X (lib. bdg.)
        1. Tubman, Harriet, 1820?–1913—Juvenile literature. 2. Slaves—United States—Biography—
Juvenile literature. 3. Afro-Americans—Biography—Juvenile literature. 4. Underground railroad—
Juvenile literature. [1. Tubman, Harriet, 1820?–1913. 2. Slaves. 3. Underground railroad. 4. Women—
Biography. 5. Afro-Americans—Biography.] I. Title. II. Series.
    E444.T82 R68 2000
    973.7'115—dc21   00-008666

Table of Contents

Slavery in America

America is often called "the land of the free."
But everyone in America was not always
free. Starting in the 1500s, about 10 million
African people were **kidnapped** from their
homes and taken to America to be sold as

Slaves
arriving
by sea

◄ Slaves working in the fields
in Alabama

slaves. Rich people in the Southern states bought slaves to work on their large farms called **plantations**.

Plantation life was horrible for slaves. They were the property of the plantation owners. Slaves had no rights. Even though they worked very hard, they were whipped and beaten.

Many slaves tried to escape to the North where most people were against slavery. One amazing woman helped many slaves to escape. Her name was Harriet Tubman. She believed in freedom for everyone.

A poster announcing slaves for sale

◄ A plantation house

Growing Up As a Slave

Harriet Tubman was born in 1820 or 1821. (Slave owners did not record slave births.) She was the youngest of eleven children. Her parents named her Araminta Ross. People called her Minty. When she was thirteen, she took her mother's name, Harriet. Her family lived in a one-room cabin in Maryland on the large plantation of Edward Brodas.

Brodas was greedy. He hired out his slaves to other families to make more money. Harriet was sent to work for a family when she was only six years old. She had to sleep on the kitchen floor and eat table scraps

◀ Many slave families lived in cabins.

with the dogs. Then Harriet helped take
care of a baby. She was often whipped.
Harriet's next job was plowing fields and
loading wagons. She liked working outside.
It was hard work, but it made her strong.

When Harriet was thirteen, she had a very
bad accident. A plantation **overseer** was
chasing a runaway slave. He threw a heavy
iron weight at the
slave, but it hit
Harriet. A bone in
her head was broken.
For the rest of her
life, Harriet suffered

This poster offers
slaves for hire.

NEGROES FOR HIRE.

AT THE COURT-HOUSE, IN THIS CITY,

On Wednesday, April 17

I will offer publicly to hire, for the balance of this year, the following
NEGROES, to wit:

LETTY, a Woman from 40 to 50 years
of age;
FRANCES, a young Woman, with her
Infant Child;
TAYLOR, a Boy about 14 years old; and
LAWSON, a Boy about 12.

The Hirers must give security, and must agree to keep the Negro
hired by him in this County, clothe well, pay medical bills, and return
on the 1st January, 1862.

Hiring at 12 o'clock, at South Gate of Court Yard.

J. E. GLEAVES, C. & M.,
Chancery Court at Nashville.

Nashville, April 9, 1861.

[Nashville Patriot Print.]

blackouts—spells in which she would suddenly fall asleep.

In 1844, Harriet married John Tubman. He was a free black man but Harriet was still a slave. She told John that she wanted to run away. John thought she was being silly because she would be punished if she were caught.

Working in the fields was back-breaking.

The Underground Railroad

Then Harriet heard that she and her brothers were going to be sold. She decided that now she had to escape. She would take the **Underground Railroad**.

The Underground Railroad wasn't a railroad at all. It was a group of people who hated slavery and wanted to help slaves escape. The homes and barns of these people were called **stations**.

Runaway slaves headed north, hiding

A runaway slave

at these stations along the way. People called **conductors** led the slaves through the woods at night. Sometimes they hid them in secret spaces in their wagons. Other times they **disguised** them for travel on steamboats or trains. The slaves had to reach one of the eighteen Northern states where slaves were free.

A portrait of Harriet Tubman

Escape to Philadelphia

In 1849, Harriet got a name and directions
to a station. She set out all by herself. She
had no money and no map. She followed the
North Star in the night sky. Luckily, she did
not hear dogs or men on horses chasing her.

The
Underground
Railroad

The ruins of a station on the Underground Railroad

She walked to the first station and hid there until it was safe to go to the next one. After a long, hard trip, she finally reached Pennsylvania. She was a free woman.

In Philadelphia, Pennsylvania, Harriet found a job as a cook at a hotel. Now that she was free, Harriet wanted to help her family get to freedom too.

◄ Philadelphia in the 1850s, about the time Harriet arrived

Brave Harriet

The Fugitive Slave Act was passed in 1850. The new law said that slaves who escaped to free states could be returned to their owners. Nowhere in the United States was safe now. To be free, slaves had to get to Canada.

Harriet was brave. She made trips back to the South and brought her sister and brother to Canada. On one trip, she found out that John had married another woman. That was a hard time for Harriet. She decided that her new role in life was to lead slaves to safety. She became a conductor on the Underground Railroad.

◄ A magazine portrait of Harriet

Helping Others to Freedom

From 1850 to 1861, Harriet made nineteen dangerous trips to help slaves escape. People called her Moses, after the man in the Bible who led his people out of slavery. At first, people thought she was a man, because they thought only a man could be so brave. A reward of $40,000 was offered for her capture.

Slaves hiding on the Underground Railroad

The trips were not easy. She and the slaves hid in swamps, wagons, and secret rooms. She had to give children a special medicine to make them sleep so that they wouldn't make any noise. Sometimes slaves got so scared that they wanted to turn back. Harriet carried a gun and forced them to go on.

Harriet was always fearless. She trusted that God would lead her and the slaves to safety. Harriet led more than 300 slaves to freedom. She also rescued her family in Maryland, including her parents. She bought her parents a house in Auburn, New York, and moved there.

The Civil War

Harriet also played an important part in the American Civil War. The Civil War (1861–1865) was fought between the North and South to end slavery. Harriet served as a nurse to soldiers. She also helped the North map out the land behind enemy lines. She helped troops free more than 750 slaves from prison.

Abraham Lincoln reads the Emancipation Proclamation to his advisers.

In 1863, President Abraham Lincoln signed the Emancipation Proclamation. It ended slavery. All black people were finally free. Two years later, the war ended, and the North won.

◄ Black troops fought to end slavery during the Civil War.

Coming Home

In 1865, Harriet returned to her house in New York. Many sick and old people came to her door, asking for food and a place to sleep. She never turned anyone away. One of these people

was Nelson Davis.
Harriet married him
in 1869. He was
sick from the war
and died in 1888.

Even though
slavery was over,
Harriet felt
strongly about other
problems. She spoke
at meetings about giving
women and blacks the

Harriet as an old woman

right to vote. She bought land for her church
to build a free home for needy black people.

◄ Harriet with black Americans in the 1890s

HARRIET TUBMAN HOME

A Hero

On March 10, 1913, Harriet died of **pneumonia**. During ninety-three years of life, she helped many people. Her bravery and faith in God led hundreds of slaves to freedom and helped end slavery in America. She was a true American hero.

◄ Harriet Tubman's home is now a museum.

Important Dates in Harriet Tubman's Life

1820–1821	Born Araminta Ross in Bucktown, Maryland
1934	Takes her mother's name, Harriet
1844	Marries John Tubman
1849	Escapes to Philadelphia, Pennsylvania
1850	Fugitive Slave Act is passed
1850–1861	Makes nineteen trips to the South and rescues more than 300 slaves
1861–1865	The North and South fight in the Civil War; works as a nurse for the army and helps free 750 slaves
1863	Emancipation Proclamation is signed
1869	Marries Nelson Davis
1903	Gives land for a home for needy black people
1913	Dies on March 10 in Auburn, New York

Glossary

conductor—a member of the Underground Railroad who led slaves to safety in the North or Canada

disguised—changed the appearance of

kidnapped—taken away forcefully

overseer—a person in charge of slave workers and punishment of slaves

plantation—a large farm

pneumonia—a disease that makes it hard to breathe; a lung disease

stations—the homes and barns where slaves escaping to the North hid safely

Underground Railroad—a group of people who helped slaves escape

Did You Know?

- Harriet Tubman once said proudly she "never lost a single passenger."

- When Harriet Tubman worked as a conductor, she used to leave on Saturday night because the slave owners couldn't put notices in the newspapers until Monday morning.

- Queen Victoria of Great Britain gave Harriet Tubman a silver medal for bravery in 1897.

Want to Know More?

At the Library

Benjamin, Anne, and Ellen Beier (illustrator). *Young Harriet Tubman: Freedom Fighter*. Mahwah, N.J.: Troll Associates, 1992.

Elish, Dan. *Harriet Tubman and the Underground Railroad*. Brookfield, Conn.: Millbrook Press, 1993.

Troy, Don. *Harriet Ross Tubman*. Chanhassen, Minn.: The Child's World, 1999.

On the Web

Africans in America

http://www.pbs.org/wgbh/aia/part4/4p1535.html

For a biography of Harriet Tubman and information about the Underground Railroad

The Underground Railroad

http://www.nationalgeographic.com/features/99/railroad/j1.html

To follow in the footsteps of slaves on the Underground Railroad

Through the Mail

The National Underground Railroad Freedom Center

312 Elm Street
20th Floor
Cincinnati, OH 45202

On the Road

The Harriet Tubman Home

180 South Street
Auburn, NY 13201
315/252-2081

Index

About the Author
Ever since Dana Meachen Rau can remember, she has loved to write. A graduate of Trinity College in Hartford, Connecticut, Rau works as a children's book editor and illustrator and has written many books for children, including biographies, nonfiction, early readers, and historical fiction. Rau lives in Farmington, Connecticut (one of the stops on the Underground Railroad), with her husband, Chris, and son, Charlie.